No More Violence in Your Home

Megan Bell

Megan Bell

Megan Bell

Copyright Page

Copyright Holder: © Megan Bell
Author: © Megan Bell 2025
Publisher: House of Gold
Release Year 2025
All Rights Reserved

All texts, illustrations, photographs, graphics, logos, and other content included in this book are the exclusive property of the author, and are protected by national and international intellectual property laws. Reproduction, distribution, public communication, transformation or any other form of exploitation of all or part of this work is strictly prohibited without the prior express written permission of the author.

Megan Bell

Index

The Broken Silence	7
Warning Signs	12
The Roots of Abuse	17
The Impact of Abuse on Children and Adolescents	22
The Invisible Face of Psychological Violence	28
Myths and Realities of Domestic Violence	34
The Consequences of Abuse on Mental Health	40
Before It's Too Late	46
Educating for Non-Violence	52
The Power of Forgiveness and Reconstruction	58
What to do if you are a Victim?	63
Supporting a Person in a Situation of Violence	69
The Role of Laws and Society	75
Changing the Paradigm	81
Testimonies of Overcoming	87
Building a New Home	93

Megan Bell

The Broken Silence

The home, that space that many of us imagine as a refuge of love, understanding and tranquility, can become, in some cases, a place of pain and suffering. In many families, violence remains hidden behind closed doors, disguised as normal arguments, "small fights" or, worse still, silenced by fear and shame. This chapter seeks to open that door, break the silence and allow the truth to come to light. Because only by facing what is happening can we begin to change it.

Domestic violence doesn't always manifest itself in obvious shouting or hitting. It often begins subtly, with hurtful words, intimidating glances, or humiliating gestures. It's easy to justify these actions at first. "It's just his character," "He's stressed out from work," "It's my fault too." However, these justifications are often the first brick in a wall that, over time, isolates victims and normalizes abuse.

It is important to understand that abuse is not limited to the physical. Insults, constant criticism, threats, excessive control, and even intentional silence are all forms of psychological violence. These actions can be just as damaging as hitting, because they erode self-esteem, generate anxiety, and make victims question their own worth. Recognizing that these behaviors are not normal or acceptable is the first step to breaking the cycle.

For those living in a violent environment, silence can become a survival mechanism. It is difficult to talk about what happens when fear dominates every aspect of life. Fear of not being believed, of being judged, of retaliation from the aggressor. Silence is often also maintained out of a desire to protect children, family, or even the aggressor himself. But this silence does not protect anyone; on the contrary, it perpetuates suffering and allows violence to continue to grow.

It is common for victims to feel that they are alone, that no one will understand what they are going through. However, this perception is not true. Many people have gone through similar situations and have managed to move forward. There are organizations, professionals and people willing to listen, to offer support and to accompany them in the process of seeking help.

Talking can be scary, but it is an act of courage that can change lives.

It is essential that those who witness or suspect domestic violence do not remain indifferent. The silence of others also contributes to the continuation of abuse. If you notice that someone close to you is experiencing abuse, offer your support in a respectful and non-judgmental way. It is not about invading people's privacy, but about being available, listening and reminding them that they are not alone.

Talking about domestic violence is not easy. Many cultures have normalized certain abusive behaviors, and breaking those patterns means facing deeply held beliefs. But change is possible. Every time someone dares to speak up, to say "this isn't right," a door is opened for others to do the same. This is a path that requires courage, but it is worth taking, because no one deserves to live in fear in their own home.

When we break the silence, we not only begin to heal, but we also send a powerful message: violence has no place in our lives. Talking about what is happening, seeking help, and speaking out when necessary are steps that can make the difference between a life full of pain and a life full of hope. Silence protects the aggressor; speech frees the victim. It is time to choose freedom.

Warning Signs

Recognizing the warning signs is crucial to detecting domestic violence before it becomes a bigger problem. These signs are often mistaken for everyday problems or justified as part of family life, but paying attention can make the difference between taking action in time or allowing the abuse to continue. This chapter is dedicated to helping you identify these signs, whether you experience them yourself or see them in someone close to you.

One of the most obvious signs is fear. If someone in the home is constantly afraid of another person, whether it's a parent, partner, or even a child, this is a red flag. This fear can manifest itself in many ways: avoiding eye contact, measuring each word before speaking, or trying to anticipate the other's needs to avoid conflict. Living in fear in your own home is not normal, and should never be accepted as an everyday occurrence.

Isolation is another important sign. People who are victims of domestic violence often withdraw from their friends and family. This may be because the abuser demands it, controlling who the victim associates with, or because the victim feels ashamed or afraid to share what they are experiencing. If someone who used to be sociable starts avoiding meetings, not responding to messages, or acting distant, they may be facing a situation of abuse.

Changes in physical appearance are also alarming. While not all violence is physical, marks on the body, such as bruises or wounds that are justified with lame explanations, should be taken seriously. Also, if someone starts wearing clothing that is not appropriate for the weather to cover up, such as long sleeves in the middle of summer, they may be trying to hide signs of violence.

Excessive control is another behavior that should not be ignored. This includes constantly monitoring where a person is, who they talk to, or what they do. An abuser may check the victim's phone, forbid them from leaving the house without permission, or handle money in a way that leaves the victim without financial independence. Although some may disguise this control as concern or love, it is not. Controlling is not caring, it is a way of exerting power over another.

Psychological abuse, while it leaves no visible scars, is just as damaging. Phrases like "you are worthless," "no one else will love you," or "it's all your fault" are forms of emotional abuse. These words, repeated constantly, destroy self-esteem and make the victim feel trapped, without the power to seek help. If someone in the home uses hurtful or humiliating words as a way to gain control, that is violence.

Changes in children's behavior should also be watched out for. Young children are often very sensitive to what is happening at home, even if they are not the direct targets of abuse. If a child becomes withdrawn, anxious, or shows fear toward a family member, he or she may be witnessing or experiencing violence. Children do not always have the words to describe what they are feeling, but their actions speak for them.

Finally, constantly justifying the abuser's behavior is a red flag. Phrases like "he just had a bad day," "that's just the way he is," or "he only gets like that when he's stressed" are ways of minimizing the abuse. Victims often use these explanations as a coping mechanism, but they are actually normalizing something that should not be accepted.

Identifying these signs isn't always easy, especially since domestic violence often develops gradually. However, if something doesn't feel right, it probably isn't. It's important to listen to your intuition and observe carefully. If you recognize any of these signs in your home or in someone close to you, don't ignore it. Talking, seeking help, or even just offering support can be the first step to changing the situation. Acting in time can save lives.

The Roots of Abuse

Abuse does not just happen. Behind every act of domestic violence there are deep roots that fuel abusive behavior. To understand why abuse occurs, it is necessary to look beyond the acts themselves and explore the causes that give rise to them. This chapter seeks to unravel those roots, because only by understanding them can we begin to prevent them.

One of the main causes of abuse is the environment in which the abuser grew up. Often, those who exercise violence were witnesses or victims of abuse in their childhood. If a child grows up seeing that conflicts at home are resolved with shouting, hitting or insults, it is likely that, when he becomes an adult, he will repeat those same patterns. This does not justify the behavior, but it does explain it. Violence can be passed down from generation to generation if it is not stopped.

Another important root is culture and social beliefs. In many societies, ideas that normalize control and dominance of one person over another still persist, especially in romantic or family relationships. Phrases such as "the man is the boss in the house" or "if he hits you, it is because he loves you" perpetuate the idea that violence is acceptable. These beliefs, when left unchallenged, create an environment where abuse can flourish without being recognized as such.

Stress and the pressures of everyday life also play a role. Financial problems, joblessness, illness, or work conflicts can create tensions at home. In some people, these tensions translate into violent behavior, because they have not learned healthy ways to manage their emotions. However, it is important to clarify that these situations are contributing factors, not excuses for abuse. We all face difficulties, but not all of us resort to violence.

Lack of emotional skills is another common root of abuse. Many people do not know how to express their emotions appropriately or how to resolve conflicts without resorting to aggression. This may be due to a lack of positive role models during their development or an upbringing that never prioritized emotional management. In these cases, abuse arises as an impulsive reaction to frustration, anger or insecurity.

The desire for control is also a central cause. In an abusive relationship, the abuser often seeks to exert power over the victim. This desire for control may stem from personal insecurities, fear of abandonment, or a distorted view of what love and respect mean. Controlling someone else may make the abuser feel a false sense of security or superiority, but in reality, what it reflects is an inability to handle their own emotional emptiness.

Alcohol or drug use is another factor that can aggravate abuse. Although not all abusers are addicts, and not all addicts are abusers, the use of these substances can intensify violent behavior. Under the influence of these substances, people often lose control of their emotions and actions, which can lead to more serious episodes of violence.

Finally, social permissiveness is a root that is not mentioned enough. When society does not report, does not act or looks the other way, it sends the message that violence is tolerated. Every time a neighbor ignores cries for help or a friend does not intervene for fear of causing discomfort, a system is strengthened that allows abuse to continue. Indifference is violence's best ally.

It is important to note that although these roots explain abuse, none of them justify it. We all have the ability to break negative patterns in our lives, regardless of our past or circumstances. Understanding the roots of abuse is not an excuse, but a tool to prevent and confront it. Identifying these factors in our lives or in our community is the first step to stopping violence before it occurs.

You cannot change what you do not understand. Therefore, this analysis of the roots of abuse is not only an exercise in reflection, but a call to action. Changing our beliefs, educating the new generations, learning to manage our emotions and, above all, not being indifferent, are actions that can make a difference. Because even if abuse has deep roots, it is always possible to tear them out and start again.

The Impact of Abuse on Children and Adolescents

The impact of abuse on children and adolescents is profound and long-lasting. Although it is often thought that children do not understand or are unaware of what is happening around them, the truth is that they are extremely sensitive to conflict and violence in the home. Even when they are not the direct victims, simply witnessing abuse among family members can mark their lives in ways that are often not immediately apparent. This chapter explores how abuse affects the youngest and why it is so important to protect them.

When a child grows up in a violent environment, their world is no longer a safe place. Home, which should be their refuge, becomes a space of fear and uncertainty. This creates constant stress in their life, known as toxic stress. Unlike the normal worries we all face, toxic stress occurs when a child lives in a continuous state of alert, waiting for something bad to happen. This type of stress can affect their brain development, damaging areas related to learning, memory, and emotional control.

On an emotional level, children who experience or witness abuse often develop feelings of guilt and shame. It is common for them to think that they are somehow responsible for the violence, that if they behaved better or were more obedient, things would be different. This emotional burden can stay with them for years, affecting their self-esteem and their ability to relate to others. In many cases, these feelings translate into problems such as anxiety, depression and self-destructive behaviors.

The impact is also evident in their behaviour. Some children become withdrawn, avoid socialising and prefer to keep their distance from others. Others, however, may react in the opposite way, becoming aggressive or defiant. These behaviours are, at their core, ways of dealing with the pain and confusion they feel. An aggressive child is not looking for trouble, they are looking for help, even if they don't know how to ask for it.

In the school setting, the effects of abuse are evident. Many children who live in violent homes have difficulty concentrating in class, fall behind in their studies, or even drop out of school. The reason is simple: it is impossible to pay attention to math or history when your mind is busy worrying about what might happen at home. In addition, the lack of emotional support at home leaves them without the tools necessary to face the challenges of learning.

In adolescence, the impact of abuse can take on more complex forms. Teens who have grown up in a violent environment often look for ways to escape the reality they live in. Some turn to drug or alcohol use, while others seek refuge in toxic relationships that repeat the patterns of abuse they have learned. It is also common for them to engage in risky behaviors, such as delinquency or leaving home, because they feel they have no other option.

But perhaps the most painful impact of abuse on children and adolescents is how it affects their view of the world and themselves. Many grow up believing that violence is an inevitable part of human relationships. This can lead them to accept abuse as normal in their own future relationships, perpetuating the cycle of violence. Others, however, become convinced that they do not deserve love or respect, which limits their chances of building a full and happy life.

It is important to understand that children learn not only from what they are told, but, above all, from what they see. If a child grows up seeing that love is expressed through shouting, hitting or insults, he or she internalizes that idea. Therefore, violence at home not only harms those who suffer it directly, but it also leaves scars on the youngest children, who are at the most vulnerable stage of their development.

However, all is not lost. Children and adolescents are incredibly resilient if they receive the right help. A safe environment, with adults who listen to them, support them, and provide unconditional love, can make a huge difference in their lives. In addition, access to psychological therapy and support programs can help them process their experiences and build healthy self-esteem.

Protecting children and adolescents from abuse is not only the responsibility of parents, but of society as a whole. Every time we act to stop violence, we are taking a step towards ensuring that future generations grow up in an environment of peace and respect. Because children are a reflection of what they see and experience. If we give them a home full of love and security, they will grow up to build a better world.

Megan Bell

The Invisible Face of Psychological Violence

Psychological violence is a silent enemy that leaves deep scars, even if they are not visible to the naked eye. Unlike a blow that may be obvious to others, emotional damage often remains hidden, even to the victim. This type of violence does not leave bruises on the skin, but it marks the mind and heart in ways that can be just as painful, or even more so. It is important to talk about this invisible face of violence, because understanding it is the first step to confronting and stopping it.

Psychological violence doesn't always start in obvious ways. It can begin with seemingly innocent comments, such as ridiculing jokes, constant criticism disguised as "honesty," or attitudes that make the other person feel inadequate. Over time, these behaviors escalate, and the victim begins to doubt themselves. Phrases like "you're worthless," "you're crazy," or "no one else will love you" become part of the routine, and the victim begins to believe them.

One of the most dangerous characteristics of psychological violence is that it is confusing. Many victims do not realize that they are being abused because there is no physical blow. It is common to hear phrases such as "but he has never hit me" or "he just has a bad temper." However, words have enormous power. They can build or destroy, and in the case of psychological violence, they are used as weapons to emotionally disarm the other person.

Control is another key tool in this type of violence. A psychological abuser seeks to have power over the victim's life, and does so in subtle but effective ways. This can include controlling who they talk to, how they dress, what decisions they make, or even how they spend their money. Often, this comes in the guise of concern or caring, such as saying "I care about you, so I want to know where you are all the time." But the reality is that this control has nothing to do with love; it is a form of domination.

Isolation is another common strategy in psychological violence. The abuser tries to cut the victim's ties with family and friends, because he knows that an isolated person is easier to manipulate. He can do this directly, by saying that such relationships are not good for him, or indirectly, by creating conflicts every time the victim tries to socialize. Over time, the victim finds himself alone, with no one to talk to or seek support from.

Psychological violence can also manifest itself in the use of silence as punishment. Ignoring the other person, not answering their questions, or treating them as if they don't exist are all forms of emotional manipulation. This type of behavior can make the victim feel like they've done something wrong, even when they haven't. It's a cruel tactic that leaves the victim in a constant state of uncertainty and anxiety.

The damage caused by psychological violence is not always immediately noticeable, but the consequences are devastating. Victims often develop low self-esteem, anxiety, depression and, in extreme cases, suicidal thoughts. Even when they manage to leave the relationship, many carry the emotional scars with them for years, feeling broken or unable to trust anyone again.

It is important to understand that psychological violence does not discriminate. It can occur in any type of relationship: between couples, parents and children, friends or even coworkers. And what is most worrying is that, because it is less visible than other forms of abuse, it often goes unnoticed, both by the victims and by those around them.

So how can you identify and deal with psychological violence? The first step is to acknowledge that something is not right. If a relationship makes you feel constantly insecure, belittled or controlled, it is time to question what is happening. Talking to someone you trust or seeking professional support can be a great help in understanding the situation and making decisions.

It is also crucial to educate ourselves and others about this type of violence. Society has to stop minimizing phrases like "it's just words" or "it's not that bad." Emotional damage is real and can be just as destructive as physical damage. Talking about it, making it visible and condemning it is essential to prevent it.

Psychological violence thrives on silence and confusion. By breaking the silence and naming what is happening, we begin to weaken its power. We all deserve relationships based on respect, love and equality, and no one should tolerate anything less. Because even though the wounds of words cannot be seen, they hurt. And they deserve to be attended to, healed and, above all, prevented.

Megan Bell

Myths and Realities of Domestic Violence

Domestic violence is a topic surrounded by myths and misunderstandings that, far from helping, often perpetuate the problem. These myths can make victims feel trapped, aggressors justify their behavior, and society in general turn a blind eye to a reality that needs to be addressed. This chapter seeks to dismantle some of the most common misconceptions about domestic violence and replace them with truths that we should all know.

One of the most widespread myths is that domestic violence occurs only in low-income or poorly educated families. The reality is that violence does not discriminate. It can occur in any type of home, regardless of economic, educational or cultural level. The abusers may be highly educated and respected people in their communities, while the victims may be seemingly strong and successful people. This myth is dangerous because it creates a false sense of security, as if certain groups are immune to the problem, when this is not the case.

Another common myth is that if the violence is not physical, it is not serious. Many people think that only hitting counts as abuse, but this is far from true. Emotional, verbal and psychological violence can be just as damaging – and even harder to overcome – because it leaves no visible marks. Hurtful words, excessive control, threats and isolation are forms of violence that deeply affect victims, often leaving them with emotional scars for life.

Domestic violence is also believed to occur because the abuser loses control. This myth suggests that abusers act on impulse or out of an inability to control their temper. The truth is that violence is not a loss of control, but a choice. The abuser chooses to exercise violence as a way to dominate and subdue the victim. This is evidenced by the fact that abusers are often selective in their behavior, acting violently only with certain people and in certain places, while behaving completely differently in other contexts.

Many victims believe the myth that the abuser will change with time or with enough love and patience. This belief leads many people to stay in abusive relationships for years, hoping for a change that rarely occurs. The reality is that change is only possible if the abuser acknowledges his or her behavior, takes responsibility, and seeks professional help. The victim's love is not enough to break the cycle of violence, because the problem is not with the victim, but with the abuser.

One particularly damaging myth is that victims of domestic violence are weak or that they enjoy abuse. Nothing could be further from the truth. Victims do not choose to be abused, nor do they enjoy violence. Often, they stay in the relationship out of fear, lack of resources, or because of the abuser's manipulations into believing they have no other choice. Judging victims rather than supporting them only reinforces their sense of isolation and hopelessness.

Another myth that is often heard is that children are not affected if they are not the direct targets of violence. The reality is that children who grow up in a violent environment suffer just as much as the direct victims. Witnessing violence leaves deep emotional scars on children, affecting their development and worldview. It also increases the risk that they themselves will become victims or aggressors in the future, perpetuating the cycle of violence.

Some people justify violence by saying that it is a private family matter and should not be interfered with. This myth has allowed family violence to persist for generations. The truth is that violence is never a private matter. It affects not only those who suffer it directly, but also society as a whole. Denouncing violence and taking action to stop it is a collective responsibility, not an intrusion.

Finally, there are those who believe that domestic violence is inevitable, that it is part of human relationships or that it has always existed and cannot be eradicated. This thinking is dangerous because it normalizes something that should not be accepted under any circumstances. Violence is not a natural part of relationships; it is a learned behavior that can and should be unlearned. With education, support, and a change in social attitudes, it is possible to reduce and eventually eliminate domestic violence.

Debunking these myths not only helps us better understand the problem, but it also empowers us to confront it. By acknowledging the realities of domestic violence, we can act more effectively to support victims, hold perpetrators accountable, and build an environment where violence has no place. Because the truth, although sometimes uncomfortable, is always the first step towards change.

The Consequences of Abuse on Mental Health

Abuse doesn't just damage the body; it deeply affects the mind and heart. The scars it leaves on mental health are real and can last for years, even a lifetime. Understanding these consequences is critical, because often those who have experienced abuse don't even realize how much it has affected their emotional well-being. This chapter explores the ways in which abuse impacts mental health and why it's so important to seek help to heal.

One of the most common consequences of abuse is anxiety. Living in an environment where there is violence, shouting, or constant manipulation creates a state of permanent alert. The abused person is always anticipating the worst, wondering when the next outburst of aggression will come. This can lead to physical symptoms such as palpitations, excessive sweating, insomnia, and a feeling of suffocation, which are often signs of an anxiety disorder. Even when the violence stops, the body and mind can remain in this state of alert, as if they were trapped in a traumatic experience that never ends.

Depression is another common consequence. Being a victim of abuse, whether physical, psychological or verbal, deeply affects self-esteem. Over time, the person begins to believe that they are worthless, that they are not enough or that they deserve what happens to them. These negative ideas become an emotional burden that is difficult to manage, which can lead to a constant feeling of sadness, hopelessness and lack of motivation to carry out daily activities. In the most severe cases, depression can lead to suicidal thoughts, because the person feels that there is no way out.

Abuse can also lead to PTSD, especially if the experiences were very traumatic or prolonged over time. People with this disorder constantly relive the moments of violence through nightmares, intrusive memories or feelings of still-present danger. This can cause them to avoid places, people or situations that remind them of what they experienced, greatly limiting their daily lives. In addition, they often have difficulty trusting others, which complicates their personal and professional relationships.

The impact of abuse on mental health is not limited to these disorders. It also affects a person's ability to handle stress and regulate their emotions. Many victims develop anger problems, difficulty controlling crying, or a constant feeling of irritability. This does not mean that they are "difficult" people, but rather that their emotional system has been so affected that it is difficult for them to respond in a balanced way to the challenges of daily life.

For those who have experienced psychological violence, the consequences can include problems with self-image and self-confidence. Hurtful words and constant criticism leave a mark that can be difficult to erase. The victim begins to doubt their abilities, their decisions, and their own worth. Even after leaving the abusive relationship, these insecurities can remain present, affecting their ability to move forward in life and achieve their goals.

It's important to mention that abuse can also lead to self-destructive behaviors. Some people turn to alcohol, drugs, or food as a way to cope with emotional pain. Others may get involved in toxic relationships or repeat patterns of abuse because they haven't received the support they need to heal. These behaviors aren't a sign of weakness, but rather a sign that the person is trying to find relief in a way that, while harmful, is the only way they know how.

Additionally, abuse can affect a person's ability to form and maintain healthy relationships. Fear of rejection, fear of being hurt again, or lack of trust can cause them to isolate themselves or choose relationships where the same patterns of abuse are repeated. This creates a cycle that is difficult to break, with the abuse continuing to influence their life long after it has ended.

It is crucial to understand that the mental health consequences of abuse are not a sign of weakness or something that victims should feel ashamed of. No one chooses to be abused, and the emotional wounds that remain are a natural response to trauma. What is most important is to know that these wounds can heal. With support, therapy, and time, many people manage to rebuild their self-esteem, regain confidence in themselves and others, and live a full and happy life.

Seeking help isn't easy, especially since abuse often comes with feelings of shame or guilt. But it's a necessary and courageous step. Talking to a therapist, trusted friend, or support group can make all the difference. Mental health is just as important as physical health, and no one should feel bad about seeking the care they need to heal.

Abuse can leave deep marks on the mind, but it does not define the people who have suffered it. Every day is a new opportunity to rebuild what has been lost, to learn to love oneself, and to discover that life can be better, free of violence and full of peace. No one deserves to live with the scars of abuse, and everyone deserves the opportunity to heal and find happiness.

Megan Bell

Before It's Too Late

Taking action before it's too late can make the difference between healing and a tragedy that could have been prevented. Domestic violence is a problem that grows in silence, fueled by fear, shame and denial. Often, those who experience or witness abuse believe they can handle it, that things will get better with time or that it's not as bad as it seems. But this is a dangerous trap. Ignoring the problem doesn't make it go away; on the contrary, it often makes it worse.

Recognizing that something is wrong is the first step, but it's not always easy. Victims often get caught in a cycle of violence that makes it difficult for them to see the situation clearly. They may justify the abuser's behavior, minimize the harm, or even blame themselves. This is one of the biggest obstacles, because until there is recognition that there is a problem, it is impossible to seek a solution. If you feel right now that something is not right in your home, listen to that inner voice that tells you so. You are not exaggerating or being weak by seeking help. You are being brave.

One of the clearest signs that action is needed is fear. If you fear the person you live with, either physically or emotionally, it is a sign that the situation is dangerous. Fear should have no place in a healthy relationship. Relationships based on respect and love do not generate terror or anxiety. If you live in fear, it is time to consider your safety as a priority.

It's important to understand that you are not alone. There are resources, people, and organizations dedicated to helping you. Often, the abuser makes the victim believe that there is no way out, that no one will believe them, or that they will not survive without them. These are lies designed to maintain control. The reality is that there are support networks, helplines, and trained professionals to guide you through this process. Seeking help is not a sign of failure; it is an act of courage and self-love.

If you're reading this and you're not a direct victim, but you know someone who might be in danger, you also have an important role to play. Many victims don't speak out because they're afraid or don't know how. If you suspect someone is being abused, offer your support in a sensitive way. Listen without judgment, offer your company, and share information about resources that can help. Sometimes a small gesture of empathy can be the push that person needs to take the first step toward a better life.

Abuse doesn't just affect the direct victim; it impacts the entire family, especially children. If there are children in the home, it's even more urgent to act. Children who grow up in a violent environment carry an emotional burden that can stay with them for life. Many develop behavioral problems, anxiety, or difficulties relating to others. But most importantly, they also learn patterns of behavior that they could repeat in the future, perpetuating the cycle of violence. By breaking this cycle, you're not only protecting yourself, but also the generations that come after you.

Waiting for things to change on their own rarely works. Time alone does not solve violence; change requires action. Talking to a therapist, going to a shelter, or even seeking legal support may seem scary at first, but they are necessary steps to ensure your safety and well-being. No matter how difficult the road may seem, it is possible to move forward and build a life free of violence.

It's crucial to plan carefully. If you decide to leave an abusive relationship, do so with a plan that prioritizes your safety. Talk to people you trust, organize important documents, and consider contacting a shelter or a domestic violence organization. These places are prepared to offer you protection and guidance during the most difficult times. Remember that no one deserves to live in fear, and there are resources designed to help you through this process.

Don't ignore the warning signs, whether in your own life or someone else's. Domestic violence doesn't go away on its own; it requires intervention. Every day that goes by without action increases the risk, both for the victim and those around them. It's best to act early, when there are still options and the possibility of getting out of the situation without irreparable consequences.

If you've come this far, it's because you're looking for answers, maybe even hope. Let me tell you that hope exists. Many people who have experienced violence have found a way out, have healed, and have discovered a new way of living. There's no reason you can't do it too. The road may be difficult, but every step you take toward your well-being is a step toward a better life. You're not alone, and it's never too late to make the decision to take care of yourself and those you love. Before it's too late, take the first step. Your future is waiting for you.

Megan Bell

Educating for Non-Violence

Education is the key to building a future free of violence. No one is born knowing how to treat others with respect or how to handle conflicts in a healthy way. All of this is learned, and that is precisely why it is so important to teach the new generations to live together without resorting to abuse. Educating for non-violence does not only mean preventing physical aggression, but also instilling values such as empathy, tolerance and assertive communication. This chapter explores how we can create positive change from home, school and community.

At home, children learn their first lessons in behavior. What they see and hear in their family environment profoundly influences how they perceive the world. If they grow up in a home where shouting, swearing, or hitting are common, they will most likely view violence as normal. That's why it's essential for parents and caregivers to become role models of respect and kindness. This doesn't mean being perfect, because no one is, but it does mean being aware of how our words and actions affect others.

The way we handle conflicts in front of children is a powerful educational tool. If we show that it is possible to resolve disagreements by talking, listening and reaching agreements, we give them a positive model to follow. On the contrary, if we react with anger or aggression, we teach them that this is the way to solve problems. Reflecting on our own behavior is not easy, but it is a necessary step in educating children in non-violence. If we make a mistake, it is also important to apologize. This shows them that even adults can make mistakes, but the most valuable thing is to recognize it and try to improve.

In schools, non-violence education should be a priority. Teachers have the opportunity to positively influence hundreds of children and young people, helping them develop life skills that go beyond math or history. Including topics such as conflict resolution, emotional intelligence and empathy in the school curriculum can make a big difference. These skills not only help prevent violence, but also prepare students to be responsible and respectful adults.

A key aspect is teaching children to identify and express their emotions. Violence often arises because people do not know how to manage feelings such as anger, frustration or fear. If children learn from a young age that it is okay to feel angry, but that there are appropriate ways to express that anger, they will be better prepared to deal with difficult situations without resorting to aggression. Simple activities such as using drawings, games or guided conversations can be effective tools to teach them how to manage their emotions.

In the community, we can also work to foster a culture of nonviolence. Community programs, awareness campaigns, and activities that promote peaceful coexistence are ways to engage people of all ages. These efforts help create an environment where violence is not tolerated and where everyone understands the importance of treating others with respect. They also reinforce the message that nonviolence is not just an individual responsibility, but a collective effort.

It is important to talk to teenagers clearly and directly about the topic of violence. At this stage of life, they are forming their identity and learning how to relate to others. Teaching them about consent, respect in relationships, and how to identify abusive behavior is crucial. It is also essential that they know where to seek help if they ever feel in danger or if they believe that someone close to them is in a risky situation.

Educating for non-violence is not just about avoiding abuse, but about building relationships based on mutual respect. This includes teaching people to communicate effectively. Assertive communication, which involves expressing our needs and opinions without being aggressive or passive, is a powerful tool for preventing conflict. By learning to listen to others and express our ideas clearly, we can reduce the misunderstandings and tensions that often lead to violence.

Another important aspect is to recognize and dismantle the cultural ideas that perpetuate violence. Often, beliefs such as "men should not show emotions" or "women should endure for the sake of the family" contribute to normalizing abuse. Challenging these ideas and promoting values of equality and respect is essential to changing the way we see and treat others.

Finally, it is important to remember that nonviolence education is not a process that is completed overnight. It is an ongoing effort that requires patience and commitment. But every small step counts. Every conversation about respect, every moment we choose to resolve conflict peacefully, every time we show empathy toward others, we are building a safer and kinder world.

Teaching people to live together without violence is a gift we give to future generations. It is the foundation for healthier relationships, stronger communities, and a more just society. Education is the most powerful weapon against violence, and we all have the power to use it to create positive change. In the end, nonviolence is not just a goal; it is a path we can take together, starting today.

Megan Bell

The Power of Forgiveness and Reconstruction

Forgiveness and rebuilding are concepts that can seem impossible after experiencing abuse. When the wounds are deep and the pain seems endless, the idea of forgiving can feel like a betrayal of oneself or something unnecessary. However, forgiveness is not for the person who hurt you; it is for you. It is a powerful act that frees you from the weight of resentment, helps you heal, and allows you to move forward toward a fuller life. This chapter does not seek to impose forgiveness, but to show how it can be a tool to rebuild your life.

Forgiveness doesn't mean forgetting what happened or justifying the actions of the person who hurt you. It also doesn't mean that you have to reconcile with that person or allow them back into your life. Forgiveness is an internal process that begins when you decide to let go of the resentment that keeps you tied to the past. It's an act of personal liberation, a gift you give yourself to stop carrying pain that doesn't belong to you.

The forgiveness process is not linear and does not happen overnight. It is completely normal to feel anger, sadness, or confusion as you work on healing. Don't force yourself to forgive if you're not ready. Taking the time to process your emotions is part of the journey. Talking to a therapist, journaling, or even meditating can be helpful tools to explore your feelings and take small steps toward forgiveness.

It's important to recognize that forgiveness doesn't always happen in a single moment. It may be a decision you make several times as you move through your healing process. There will be days when you feel like you've put the pain behind you, and other days when memories come back and make you question whether you've really made it. This is normal and doesn't mean you're failing; it's simply part of the rebuilding process.

Rebuilding your life after abuse takes courage and commitment. Many people feel like they have lost a part of themselves because of the violence they have suffered, but it is possible to recover what seemed lost. Rebuilding begins with small steps, such as setting personal goals, surrounding yourself with supportive people, and working on strengthening your self-esteem. Each small step forward is a victory that brings you closer to a freer and more fulfilling life.

Forgiveness can also be directed at yourself. Many victims of abuse carry feelings of guilt, thinking that they somehow provoked the abuse or that they could have prevented it. These thoughts are common, but they are not true. No one deserves to be abused, and no action justifies violence. Forgiving yourself is an act of self-love that allows you to let go of blame that does not belong to you and recognize that you did the best you could in a difficult situation.

Rebuilding also involves learning to trust again, both in yourself and in others. This isn't easy, especially if the abuse came from someone close to you, such as a family member or partner. But with time and the right support, you can begin to build healthier relationships based on respect and understanding. Learning to set clear boundaries and communicate your needs is critical to avoiding falling into patterns of abuse in the future.

Forgiveness and rebuilding are not signs of weakness, but of strength. They require looking inward, facing your fears, and deciding that you deserve better. It is a path full of challenges, but also opportunities to grow and rediscover who you are. Allow yourself to dream of a life free of violence and work every day to make it a reality.

There are times when it may feel like the pain is too much to overcome. In those times, remember that you are not alone. There are people who love you, who believe in you, and who are willing to support you. Don't be afraid to ask for help or to accept the hand someone offers you. Healing doesn't mean doing everything on your own; it means surrounding yourself with love and compassion as you rebuild what the abuse tried to destroy.

The power of forgiveness and rebuilding lies in its ability to transform suffering into strength. It's not about erasing the past, but about learning from it and using those lessons to create a better future. It's a process that takes time, effort, and patience, but the rewards are enormous. In the end, forgiveness and rebuilding not only free you from the weight of pain, but also allow you to rediscover peace, joy, and love in your life.

What to do if you are a Victim?

If you are a victim of abuse, the first thing you need to know is that you are not alone and it is not your fault. No one deserves to be treated with violence, whether physical, emotional, verbal or of any kind. Accepting that you are in an abusive situation can be a difficult step, but it is the first step towards freedom and recovery. This chapter is designed to guide you, give you tools and remind you that there is hope, even in the darkest of times.

The first step is to acknowledge and accept what is happening. Many people minimize or justify their abuser's behavior, thinking that things will get better or that what is happening is not so serious. But if you feel constantly in danger, if you live in fear, or if your needs and emotions are ignored or manipulated, it is important to understand that this is not normal or healthy. Recognizing that you are in an abusive relationship is not easy, but it is the beginning of change.

Safety should be your number one priority. If you feel like your life is in danger, seek help immediately. Contact law enforcement, a shelter for victims of violence, or a support organization.

Victims often feel trapped, but there are resources designed to help you. In many countries, there are 24-hour helplines where you can speak to trained people who understand your situation and can offer guidance.

If you're not in an immediate emergency situation, but you know you need to leave, it's important to plan carefully. Make sure you have access to important documents, such as your ID, birth certificates, passports, and any other essential papers. Keep some money on hand if possible, and prepare a bag with clothes and basic items you might need if you decide to leave suddenly. Talk to someone you trust, such as a close friend, family member, or even a neighbor, and share your plan with them.

Seek emotional support. Abuse affects not only your body, but also your mind and spirit. It's normal to feel confused, scared, or even guilty. Talking to someone you trust can ease some of that burden. If you have access to a therapist or counselor, consider seeking their help. They are trained to help you process your emotions and direct you to the resources you need. If you can't afford therapy, there are many organizations that offer free or low-cost services for victims of violence.

Don't underestimate the power of community. There are many individuals and groups dedicated to helping those facing abuse. Joining a support group can be incredibly helpful, as it allows you to connect with others who have been through similar experiences. Knowing that you are not alone and hearing the stories of those who have managed to move forward can give you the strength and courage you need to make important decisions.

It's important to remember that you don't owe your abuser anything. Many victims feel they have to stay out of obligation, fear of retaliation, or because they believe it's their responsibility to "fix" the situation. But your first responsibility is to yourself and, if you have children, to their well-being. You don't have to put up with abuse or sacrifice your happiness to stay in a relationship that hurts you.

If you have children, keep in mind that they are also being affected by violence, even if they are not the direct targets of abuse. Children who grow up in violent homes may develop emotional problems, difficulty trusting others, and even repeat patterns of abuse in the future. Protecting your children is another powerful reason to seek an outlet. Talk to them in an open, age-appropriate manner, and let them know that what is happening is not their fault.

When leaving an abusive relationship, it's common to feel fear or uncertainty about the future. This is normal, but it's important to remember that you deserve a better life. Freedom can feel scary at first, especially if you've been isolated or controlled for a long time. But every day you spend out of that situation is a step toward recovery and building a happier, more secure life.

Don't let abuse define who you are. You are so much more than the difficult experiences you've been through. You are strong, brave, and capable of getting through this. There will be good days and bad days in your healing process, but the important thing is that you are moving forward. Surround yourself with supportive and loving people, and work on regaining your self-confidence. Little by little, you will begin to rediscover peace, joy, and freedom.

Finally, remember that seeking help is not a sign of weakness, but of courage. By doing so, you are saying that you deserve more, that you deserve to be treated with dignity and respect. And that is absolutely true. There is a better life waiting for you, and it is never too late to reach it. Take action, seek support, and trust that you can move forward. Your well-being and happiness are worth every effort.

Supporting a Person in a Situation of Violence

Supporting someone who is experiencing violence can be one of the most important things you do in your life. Often, people in these circumstances feel alone, trapped, or unable to ask for help. Knowing how to act effectively can make the difference between staying stuck in abuse or finding a way out. This chapter is dedicated to giving you tools and guidance so that you can be a real support for someone who is experiencing this difficult situation.

The first thing you need to understand is that violence is not always visible. Many people think that abuse is limited to hitting, but emotional, verbal and psychological violence can also be devastating. If someone close to you shows signs of anxiety, fear or isolation, or if you notice drastic changes in their behavior, they could be facing a situation of violence. Pay attention to the signs and, above all, trust your intuition. If you feel that something is not right, it probably is not.

When you approach the person, do so from a place of empathy and non-judgment. Phrases like, "Why are you still there?" or "If I were you, I would have left already" aren't helpful. In fact, they can make the person feel ashamed or shut down even more. Instead, use words that show your support and concern. For example, you might say, "I've noticed you're going through a difficult time, and I'm here for you," or "I want you to know that I'm here for you if you need to talk."

Listen without interrupting. Sometimes all a person needs is someone who will listen without judgment or unsolicited advice. Let them express what they're feeling at their own pace and avoid pressuring them to share more than they're ready to share. Your role at this point is not to solve their problem, but to be a sympathetic ear and show them that they're not alone.

It's crucial to respect a person's decisions, even if you don't agree with them. Often, victims of violence aren't ready to leave their abuser because of fear, financial or emotional dependence, or because they think things will get better. While it can be frustrating to see someone stay in a harmful relationship, your support is more valuable if you respect their process. You can continue to offer help and resources without imposing your opinions or trying to control their decisions.

Offer helpful information in a gentle way. The person may not know that there are resources and organizations that can help them. However, rather than overwhelming them with too much information, you can start with something simple. For example, you could say, "I know a place that helps people in situations like yours. If you ever want more information, I can help you contact them." It's also a good idea to have helpline numbers or shelter addresses on hand in case they decide to act.

Helping doesn't mean doing everything for the person. It's natural to want to protect them and solve the problem completely, but it's important for them to feel capable of making decisions and regaining their autonomy. Your role is to support them, not to take control of their life. Accompany them in their process, but let them set the pace and decide the steps to follow.

If the person decides they want to leave the relationship, help them plan a safe exit. This can include identifying a safe place to stay, preparing important documents, and making sure they have access to money or transportation. Leaving a violent situation can be dangerous, especially if the abuser suspects something is going on. Help them create a discreet plan and consider possible risks.

It's important to remember that supporting someone in a violent situation can be emotionally draining. Make sure you're looking out for your own well-being, too. Talking to a professional or trusted friend about your own feelings can help you manage the emotional strain that comes with these types of situations. Don't feel guilty about needing support for yourself; by doing so, you'll be better equipped to help the other person.

Sometimes it may be necessary to seek outside help. If you feel that the person is in imminent danger, do not hesitate to contact the authorities or a specialized organization. However, it is important to do so in a way that does not put the victim at risk. If you decide to involve third parties, make sure that it is with the person's safety as the absolute priority.

Finally, never underestimate the power of your emotional support. Knowing that someone cares and is willing to help can be a turning point for the person experiencing violence. Even if you don't see immediate results, your constant presence and willingness to help can be the spark that motivates them to seek a better life.

Remember that you can't save someone who isn't ready to be helped, but you can be a source of support and hope. Sometimes, that's all it takes for a person to find the strength to change their situation. Stay patient, listen with your heart, and never underestimate the positive impact you can have on someone else's life. Your support can be the beginning of their journey to freedom and healing.

The Role of Laws and Society

Laws and society play a fundamental role in preventing, addressing and eradicating domestic violence. Although violence occurs in the private sphere, it is not an issue that should be resolved silently within the walls of the home. It is a problem that affects the entire community and requires a solid legal framework and a committed society to effectively address it. Understanding how laws work and how society can act collectively is key to building a safe and fair environment for all.

The legal framework in many countries has advanced considerably in recent years. There are specific laws that seek to protect victims of domestic violence, guarantee them access to justice and offer them resources to escape dangerous situations. These laws not only penalize the aggressors, but also establish mechanisms to prevent abuse and educate the population on the subject. However, for these laws to work, it is crucial that they are applied efficiently and that victims are aware of their rights.

One of the main problems that victims face is fear or distrust of the authorities. Often, they feel that their complaints will not be taken seriously or that the legal system will not be able to protect them. This is where the importance of a society that supports and backs victims comes in, encouraging them to report and helping them understand that the law is on their side. Reporting is not only a step towards justice, but also a way to prevent future acts of violence by holding the aggressor accountable for his actions.

The legal system is not perfect, and victims often face barriers such as lengthy processes, bureaucracy, or lack of resources to access lawyers and psychological support. Therefore, it is essential that laws are accompanied by programs that offer practical help to those affected. This includes shelters, helplines, financial assistance, and free access to legal services. More and more organizations are working together with governments to ensure that these resources reach those who need them.

On the other hand, laws alone are not enough. We need a society that actively rejects violence and works to change the cultural norms and attitudes that perpetuate it. In many communities, domestic violence is still seen as a private problem that should not be discussed publicly. This kind of mentality protects abusers and leaves victims isolated. To combat this, it is essential that as a society we talk openly about violence, denounce it and support those who face it.

Education is a powerful tool in this process. From an early age, we must teach children about respect, empathy, and equality. Openly talking about topics such as peaceful conflict resolution, consent, and mutual respect can prevent future generations from perpetuating cycles of violence. In addition, educating adults on how to identify and respond to situations of abuse is equally important. We all have a role to play, whether as parents, teachers, friends, or community members.

A crucial aspect of society's role is the creation of support networks. When victims know they are not alone, that there are people willing to help, and that resources are available, they are more likely to seek help. Support networks can include not only friends and family, but also community organizations, support groups, and concerned neighbors. Every small act of support can make a big difference in the life of a person facing violence.

It is also necessary for us as a society to question and challenge the structures that allow violence to persist. This includes addressing issues such as machismo, traditional gender roles and economic inequalities that often contribute to abuse. Domestic violence does not occur in a vacuum; it is influenced by the social, cultural and economic dynamics around us. If we want to eradicate it, we must be willing to analyze and change these factors.

It is important to note that society's role is not limited to reacting when violence occurs. It also includes active prevention. This means participating in awareness campaigns, supporting initiatives that promote equality, and being alert to signs of abuse in our environment. Acts of violence can often be prevented if we intervene in time, either by offering direct help or alerting the authorities.

Ultimately, laws and society must work hand in hand. Laws set the foundation for a fair and safe society, but their effectiveness depends on the collective commitment of all of us. Denouncing violence, supporting victims, educating future generations and promoting respect and equality are essential steps to creating a world where family violence has no place.

As individuals, we must not underestimate our power to bring about change. Every action, however small, can contribute to building a more compassionate and conscious society. Change begins with each of us, in our homes, in our communities and in the way we treat others. It is our collective responsibility to ensure that laws are respected, that victims find support and that domestic violence is eradicated at its root. Only in this way can we guarantee a safer and more humane future for all.

Changing the Paradigm

Changing the paradigm of family violence requires a profound transformation in the way we understand and address this problem. Violence does not arise out of nowhere; it is rooted in beliefs, cultural norms and patterns of behaviour that have been perpetuated for generations. This change is not only about eradicating physical violence, but also about building a society based on respect, equality and empathy. To achieve this, we must question our preconceived ideas, rethink our actions and create a new path towards peaceful coexistence.

For too long, domestic violence has been viewed as a private matter, something that stays "within the four walls of the home." This mindset has allowed abuse to persist in silence, protected by a wall of taboos and stigmas. Changing the paradigm begins with breaking down that wall and recognizing that domestic violence is a social problem that affects us all. When we understand that the well-being of a family directly influences the health and progress of an entire community, we understand the urgency to act.

One of the most important steps is to abandon cultural and social justifications that normalize violence. Phrases like "that's just their nature," "relationship problems are normal," or "that's how you raise your children" perpetuate an environment where abuse is tolerated or even encouraged. To change this landscape, we need to educate ourselves and others. This includes questioning rigid gender roles that dictate how men and women should behave, and challenging the idea that control or aggression are acceptable ways to resolve conflict.

Education plays a central role in this paradigm shift. From an early age, we must teach children values such as respect, equality, and peaceful conflict resolution. This does not mean just talking about these issues, but modeling them in our daily actions. Children learn by observing, and when they see relationships based on cooperation and mutual support, they adopt these behaviors as the norm. In turn, we must offer them tools to express their emotions in a healthy way, something that is often neglected in parenting.

Change also requires a broader approach to shared responsibility. Often, the burden of preventing violence falls solely on victims, who are encouraged to "leave the situation" or "get help." However, eradicating violence is a task that involves everyone. Friends, neighbors, coworkers, and family members all have a role to play in watching for signs of abuse, offering support, and taking action when necessary. We cannot remain passive bystanders; we need to become an active community that rejects violence in all its forms.

Part of shifting the paradigm is recognizing that violence affects not only those who suffer it directly, but also the entire society. The costs of family violence are reflected in mental health problems, economic hardship, lost productivity, and a generational impact that perpetuates cycles of abuse. By addressing violence as a structural problem, we can focus on solutions that benefit everyone, from strengthening community support networks to implementing effective public policies.

It is essential to work to eliminate the stigma associated with seeking help. Many victims do not report violence or do not seek support because they fear being judged or because they feel ashamed. Changing the paradigm means creating an environment where asking for help is seen as a courageous act, not a sign of weakness. This requires raising awareness in society and training institutions to respond appropriately and empathetically to those who reach out for help.

Communication is also a powerful tool in this process of change. Talking openly about domestic violence, both in the media and in our everyday conversations, helps to make the problem visible and demystify it. When we share stories, discuss solutions and question the norms that perpetuate abuse, we contribute to creating a culture of awareness and rejection of violence.

On this path to change, we cannot ignore the power of laws and public policies. These should not only focus on punishing the aggressors, but also on preventing violence and protecting victims. However, laws alone cannot bring about change. They need to be backed by a society that demands their enforcement and by resources that ensure that victims can access justice and support.

Finally, changing the paradigm means having hope. Although the problem of domestic violence is enormous and complex, it is not insurmountable. Every action, however small it may seem, contributes to a greater change. When we decide to educate our children in respect, offer a helping hand to someone in need or raise our voice against violence, we are being part of the solution. Change does not happen overnight, but with collective effort and constant commitment, we can build a world where violence has no place.

This new paradigm is not just about eliminating abuse, but about building a society where relationships are based on love, respect and equality. It is an ambitious, but necessary challenge. Each of us has a role to play in this process, and together we can transform not only our families, but also our communities and ultimately the world we live in. The real revolution begins at home, with every choice we make and with every step we take towards a future free of violence.

Testimonies of Overcoming

Testimonies of success have the power to inspire, educate and give hope. Hearing the stories of those who have faced domestic violence and found a way to rebuild their lives reminds us that it is possible to emerge from difficult situations and start anew. These real-life experiences connect us to our shared humanity, showing us that although the road may be hard, we are not alone in the struggle and there is always a light at the end of the tunnel.

One of the stories that has a profound impact is that of Ana, a woman who lived for years in a relationship marked by emotional abuse. Her partner never raised a hand against her, but his words were like knives that cut into her self-esteem. He constantly made her feel inadequate, criticized every aspect of her life, and isolated her from her friends and family. Ana came to believe that she did not deserve anything better. But one day, something changed. Upon hearing a friend talk about her own experience of emotional abuse, Ana realized that what she was experiencing was neither normal nor deserved. With the support of that friend, she sought therapy and began to build a new life, far from abuse. Now, Ana helps other women identify the signs of emotional abuse and find the courage to leave those relationships.

Then there's the case of Carlos, who grew up in a violent home. As a child, he witnessed his father beat his mother and how she endured the abuse without speaking about it. Carlos grew up fearful and resentful, believing that was the only way to live. During his teens, he began to repeat his father's patterns, reacting with anger and violence in his relationships. But everything changed when he had his first child. Seeing his little boy filled him with a love he'd never felt before and made him wonder what kind of example he wanted to be for him. Carlos sought professional help, attended support groups, and learned to manage his emotions. Today, he's an advocate for positive parenting and works in his community teaching other parents how to break the cycle of violence.

There is also the story of Mariana, a young mother who found herself trapped in an abusive relationship at a very young age. Her partner controlled her completely, from what she wore to who she spoke to. Mariana felt trapped, especially since she was financially dependent on him and feared retaliation if she tried to leave. But one day, while attending a community talk about family violence, she heard something that changed her life: the idea that she deserved to live without fear. With the help of a social worker, Mariana found a women's shelter and began rebuilding her life from scratch. She now works as a counselor at that same shelter, helping other women find their strength and their path to freedom.

The testimonies also include stories of entire communities coming together to support victims and prevent violence. In a small town, a group of neighbours decided to form a support network after the tragic death of a woman at the hands of her partner. They created a safe space where people could talk, ask for help and receive guidance. Thanks to this initiative, many families managed to get out of abusive situations before it was too late. These kinds of stories teach us that solidarity and working together can make a difference.

Each testimony is unique, but they all share something in common: the courage to face adversity and the desire to build a better life. These stories show us that no matter how dark the situation may seem, there is always a way out. Sometimes, that way out begins with a small step, such as telling someone what you are going through or seeking information about available resources. Other times, it requires a collective effort, such as the support of friends, family, and organizations dedicated to helping.

It is important to remember that moving on does not mean forgetting what happened, but rather learning to live beyond the pain. Many people who have overcome domestic violence have found ways to transform their experiences into something positive, whether by helping others, advocating for changes in the law, or simply sharing their story to inspire those still in the struggle.

Testimonies not only inspire, they also educate. Hearing these stories can help those who have not experienced violence better understand the impact it has and the importance of not judging victims. It can teach them to be more compassionate and to act as allies rather than critics. Additionally, testimonies can demystify many of the misconceptions about family violence, showing that it does not discriminate and can affect anyone, regardless of age, gender or economic status.

For those in the midst of violence, these testimonies offer hope. Knowing that others have gone through the same thing and have managed to move forward can be the push they need to take the first step toward change. Knowing that they are not alone and that there are people willing to help them can make the difference between despair and determination.

If you are experiencing violence or know someone who is, remember that there are resources available and that there are always people willing to help. Violence does not define who you are or determine your future. Stories of overcoming violence are proof that recovery is possible and that we all deserve a life full of respect, love and dignity. These stories are a reminder that, although the road may be difficult, it is never impossible. Hope, support and change are within reach.

Megan Bell

Building a New Home

Building a new home after living in a violent environment is not just a physical task of finding a place to live; it is an emotional, mental and spiritual process. It is about creating a space where peace, respect and love reign, where each member of the family can feel safe and valued. It is not an easy path, but it is deeply transformative. This chapter focuses on how to take those steps to start over and build a home that is a refuge and not a source of pain.

The first step is to recognize that the past does not define your future. Even though you have had difficult experiences, you are not doomed to repeat them. Building a new home means letting go of old patterns and committing to creating a different life. This does not mean forgetting what happened, but learning from it. Reflecting on what you want and don't want in this new stage will help you establish a clear vision of what you want your home to be like.

A new home begins with small decisions. It may be choosing a place where you feel calm, surrounded by an environment that inspires trust. But it is also about establishing basic rules that promote respect and communication. For example, deciding that there will be no shouting or insults in your home, or that differences will be resolved through dialogue, are steps that make a big difference. These decisions, although they may seem simple, lay the foundation for a safe and healthy space.

It's important to understand that rebuilding isn't just for you, but also for those who share your home. If you have children, they will also need to heal and adjust to this new stage. Talking to them, listening to them, and validating their emotions is essential. Children who have lived in a violent environment may feel insecure or afraid of change, but with time and the right support, they can learn that home doesn't have to be a place of conflict. Involving them in small decisions, such as decorating a room or choosing family activities, can help them feel part of the process and develop a sense of belonging.

Another important aspect is communication. A healthy home is built on a foundation of talking and listening. This means creating an environment where everyone feels comfortable expressing their feelings without fear of being judged or attacked. Effective communication isn't always easy, especially if you're used to keeping your emotions to yourself or reacting defensively. But with practice and patience, it's possible to improve. Consider establishing regular times to talk, such as during dinner or before bed. These spaces can become valuable moments to strengthen family ties.

Rebuilding also involves taking care of yourself. After facing violence, it's common for people to focus on surviving and forget about their own needs. However, to build a healthy home, it's essential to keep yourself well. This includes taking care of your physical and mental health, seeking support if you need it, and giving yourself permission to rest and enjoy life. Remember that you can't take care of others if you don't take care of yourself.

A home isn't just made up of walls, furniture, and decor. It's also filled with the relationships, values, and experiences you share with others. Creating family traditions can be a powerful way to strengthen the connection between household members. These traditions don't have to be complicated or expensive. They can be as simple as cooking together on the weekends, going for a walk on Sundays, or having a board game night. The important thing is that they reflect the values and joy you want for your family.

It's normal to feel unsure or have doubts about what this new stage will be like at first. You may find yourself questioning whether you're doing the right thing or fearing repeating past mistakes. These feelings are part of the process and shouldn't discourage you. Remember that building a home is an ongoing effort, and you don't have to do everything perfectly from day one. The important thing is to stay committed to improving and learning along the way.

As you move forward, you may face challenges. There will be days when old wounds seem to reopen or when you feel like you're going backwards. In those times, it's crucial to remember why you started this process and focus on the progress you've made, no matter how small. Surrounding yourself with supportive and encouraging people can also make a big difference. This includes friends, family, neighbors, or even support groups who understand what you're going through.

A final but essential aspect is forgiveness. Not just forgiveness toward those who hurt you, but also toward yourself. It's easy to fall into the trap of self-criticism and blame yourself for not having done things differently in the past. But to build a new home, you need to free yourself from that weight. Forgiveness doesn't mean justifying what happened, but allowing yourself to move forward without resentment controlling your life.

Building a new home is more than a physical act; it is an act of hope and love. It is the conscious decision to create a space where wounds can heal, where dreams can flourish, and where relationships are based on respect and equality. It is a journey that requires time, effort, and patience, but every step you take toward that goal is worth it. In the end, you will not only be creating a different home, you will be building a life that reflects the best of you and those you love. A life that is proof that even after the strongest storms, it is possible to find calm and start anew.

Megan Bell

www.ingramcontent.com/pod-product-compliance
Ingram Content Group UK Ltd.
Pitfield, Milton Keynes, MK11 3LW, UK
UKHW040724190225
455309UK00001B/19